SEEING THING

SEEING THING

EVAN FOWLER

POEMS

atmosphere press

To

Kevin

John

Bob Chisholm
oldest friend, best reader

Jonathan Topazian
poet and saint

Onlie Begetters

CONTENTS

Dreaming In Hieroglyphs

Waves, an eye, the sun: may I see
your face forever. The geese above
mean "never from today"
but we ignore them. Not every sign is true.

Blue pennants rouse the Royal bee:
the sky is blue and stays eternally,
longer than a king can stay.
Then geese return, cool in the arms of night.

which means nothing is bright,
not the sun, not love.
And a hill the sun can't climb:
darkness. Dark-time.

Entourage

I could let them all go, the letters, pencils,
hands, and scheming numerals;
only they and I would feel a difference.
I would still sit here alone late with water

early with coffee, wrestling quiet
and little stacks of terror.
At most the Ark would be short a mosquito.
Everything else is splintering out there,

chewed by the wind,
why not let them go too?
Tomorrow is New Year's day,
the day after that rent's due,

a week after that I get paid.
If I play silent games that make quiet
bearable, praying to nothing sometimes overheard,
only they and I feel a difference.

Out there dreaming in a black freeze
--know who that is? It's them,
the carnival masks a day after
spattered with glitter, food and blood. Don't be afraid,

they just want in, a little warmth,
a space to know a moment from another.
Their faces are perfect ohs of need.
My secrets are safer with them

than stones, and when warmed
they say things I wouldn't tell God if He asked,
things unsayable except by a fire
on nights like this fifty years after

with all names changed, all referents
repainted in made-up alphabets,
the fussy tessera, firmly glued in backward,
safely hidden under one face.

There's no point in saying things are bad,
they're bad everywhere.
Your pain trumps mine, mine yours, and if we scream
God deaf with the neighbors He'll move away too.

Yet this early these dark days
groaning with a grabbing chill
glaring through the window
sometimes I need to scream,

just toss my head back and exit through the mouth.
That's when I let in the handkerchief ghosts,
the humiliated totems,
and cradle them in coffee-warm hands,

all such good company, so much worse off than me.

Letter

You never opened me;
you think my name a message,
my address a history. Both could change
and then what would I mean,
what brought me here?

I came a long way; you have no idea
what it cost, what I still pay.
Soon you will scoop me out
to hold small memories or burn me
—and either will be better than this,

a drawer so dark
I can barely read myself.
Even incomprehension
would be something,
a blurred life like dreams,

more than I have. But you --
from here I can't tell if you are traveling
or had a seizure in the tub
or if in other rooms you press
letter after letter to your breast.

Pencil and Hand

I bleed meaning onto the world,
my trail a dark dancing
driven as a honey-bee's;
I skate myself out forever,
announcing my every move
is a message.
I have written "I love you more
than life" and "because you are crazy
that's why, stay gone", I do bills,
I work sums, I say and say
rubbing my face on Earth
that can only erase me by eating itself.
I salaam into space as into the sun
and etch it.

I wish you could see me all at once
I am an explosion,
my lines exulting vines, black flash
twisted as a Pict cufflink.
You cannot imagine it,
you are less alive,
more like a tree than a pencil,
with nothing much in you to say,
no visible trail. It will be hard for you,
blind hand I have carried
so long, that clings to me
with such tenderness, so trustingly,
when I have finally sung myself out,
worked my finger to the bone.

Ennead

Once, 5 decided to be 4.
Things would have been fine if 5
had gone on being 4 reporting as 5,
but he made a point of going around
taking everyone down a peg.
5 made 9 8, 10 9;
everyone had to change clothes
and big numbers started to creak
--they shouldn't jump about.

4 was so embarrassed she went on a cruise.
Finally 2 and 3 said well, OK, we are 5.
5 went to 1 and complained.
1 said why are you unhappy? After all
you aren't 5 anymore. Those days are over.
Take some time off, I'm going to.
And 1 decided to be zero.
That shut 5 up for good. He went home.
His temperature dropped to zero.
The stars went out.

4 came back and went to 6, 7, 8,
all of them, saying I had no part in this,
how could you think I would do that?
But 1 had voted for a stressless universe
and 6, 7, 8 and the others
were all zero now. 4? What is 4?
they said. Why be different?
Because I have not forgotten myself,

there are four 1s inside me,
not a row of dead eggs like in you.
I am 9's backbone, I am 10's mother
whether anyone knows me or not.

She went to 5's house. 5 was very calm.
Why were you playing such crazy-family games she asked
crying. 5 just sat there, an empty seed.
There were five zeros curled up inside him, sleeping.
Go away he said, if I ruined everything
I don't remember; forgive me,
I was who I was.

4 went to 1. His palace
was an aquarium now.
1 was floating inside, a zero.
What have you done she said.
If I ever knew, he said, I don't know now.
I was tired of the job,
having to hear it all
being alone
I don't remember
but I always thought I could bear it
and found I was wrong.
I don't let anything get to me now,
I am shaped to deflect the universe
not stand still and be built on forever.
My Lady left him there at the bottom of his lake.
Some say she took the old King's eye
but it was missing already;
he was an empty socket.

On the shore she wept and tried
not to think about what must happen.
Then she pulled herself open, pulled out
one of her 1s, and suffered herself
to be 5.
        In the days of his power
5 was an elegant numeral,
very thin or tall or both;
My Lady made him fat
or put him on his knees
or both, and he's still that way.
She tore out another 1 to make 5 6,
wincing at the resemblance.
The stone scream of 7 was her curse on 1,
head lowered in shame. But in his face
she saw herself, and loved 7.
Now she had one 1 left inside her,
a fossil idea,
the place you stand when you're dreaming.

But it was still a barely-rebuilt
world. She could be 9 (5
took orders now) and 10, and 8
if she kissed herself in a mirror,
2 if she shut one eye. But there was no 3.
That was a flaw in the universe; pi would do badly,
there would be problems up and down the line.
So she told 5, 6, and 7 it was her birthday,
could her 1s please visit. And they came
together to her door. She gave them each

10

a coat; when she buttoned them in
it was one coat. Now the world could spin,
light would find its speed,
hearts know what comes next.

The 1 inside her was lonely
for his brothers. You were always alone
she said, admit it. The world before
was only you in your eyes,
you never emptied yourself
it was simple accretion, just more you,
a coral reef of angels
with your name and address.
We have you by inference, like God,
doubly so since you're gone.
And she left him there, she never let him out,
old bad rumor, sneaky tumor.

Permanent Relocation

A little plant god is lost.
I've forgotten where I am! he cries.
Where is my place of fur,
where are the things only I explain?

On his own, off the mythic track,
he doesn't know what to do,
whether blinking is safe.
He weeps white beans and cornflowers.

Nowhere a groove his feet slide into,
no basin for flowers, milk and blood.
Where is my fume-bath?
This is yesterday's realia!

Look my obsidian feathers are twisted,
I am baffled to be in this face.
O heavens I miss being idolized!
It's good to be home among familiar things,

good to be whispered to in the dark,
good to be cherished, not lost out here
staring up at sweet grass,
presence boiling off in vines.

Lost gods are out of luck;
he'll never get back.
His priests will keep washing and kissing
an image he'll soon forget the name of.

What happens there under the weeds
he'll forget too, and then every
thing, one by one,
grain of sand to the sun, 'til he's done.

North Of North

At the North Pole head North,
spinning counter to the Earth's rotation.
When you turn past turning it's all clear,
the world is information:

look and know. That gleam on the snow
mid-between toenail and sky
is all your childhood. And here's your wife,
herself a child. If you want to die

you're well-prepared already,
and here comes high school, one more reason.
Now you are mid-season,
you and she, weathering toward each other,

comets racing in a dark nursery,
and what glitters in the blaze are all
the ways you trickled quietly
together, indirectly as leaves fall.

and now you've met and married her,
traced every talisman in trance,
and of late come North of North to scream
your life out in a blizzard and dance.

Falling Through A Wall On Glue

It happened to Richie.
When he told me in '72 I was on hash, Castaneda
and Lao Tzu and it seemed possible: slip,
lick emptiness, pass through...

I know he was inside outside
in a fall, but bad sugar
makes me fall a mile
straight down from skin in. Glue --
chisel-punch to the brain,
that'll make you go boom or why do it?
Many things could explain
what happened,
only one of them insane.

Once I lay face-down in a parking lot
with car wheels hissing by my cheeks
standing up talking to a dead friend
knowing, as we spoke, I was lying
face-down in a dark parking lot
from just the slightest dose of Too Much.
I can say this and be misunderstood.
But Richie meant it: something happened.

Later that day something happened,
the one really odd event in my life.
My room was far down a long hall,
last door on the right. It had no key,
just a combination lock on a hinge.

I opened the lock and went in,
carrying it inside,
and we smoked a genial bowl.
This took only minutes.
Then we decided to go to his room
to hear a new album, and --
I'd lost the lock. Impossibly, no place
to hide it but gone even so.
Finally I let it go
and we walked way down to his room
and he unlocked his door
and there six feet in front of us....

The best guess is, one of us
must for some reason have transported
it in the twinkling of an eye
and both of us then
for some reason forgot. No.
I know what did and didn't happen.

Our Lady of Aschaffenburg
is my sole witness now
to something that occurred and couldn't have,
a lock moved and not moved.
I must and can't be wrong and
She understands, She's wise about boundaries.
She watched over me
a hundred times when respiration
dove to a drone;
twice She walked Richie through stone.

Rehearsal

The deer that crosses Leander Road
remembers future light in its eyes
learned in dreams: it stands in the road
swallowed by light, a man laughs in shock,

it wakes shuddering. And in his warm bed
he trains too, he runs in oversize shoes
to his car but it's not his car.
Called to, it leaves with another man!

Enraged, he steals a car and goes
tearing down dark Leander Road,
black thread in a black room,
and the moon wobbles, ready to drop.

Tour

I stand by a pond that reflects
the gold light of late morning:
my feet hang from the sky.

Two men are frantically swimming to me
yelling with throats full of water,
desperate to tell me something

but I am in the British Museum
now and can't help them. Looking at
a model of the Titanic

I think of them in the other room
of the dream, choking
on foam. Should I go back?

The new metal used in the new
unsinkable Titanic is admirable, steel
lighter than a cloud. It's darker here,

marmoreal, chill. They are still
screaming. The sun will set at noon.
Maybe that's what they want to say.

In Heaven

Your room will be warm, that tiny attic room
with the John and Yoko 'War Is Over' ad from the *Tribune*,
blue plastic typewriter, Greek tourist charm of straw,
so warm my clothes melt
at the door. Help me thaw;

I promise this time to peel off each welt
instead of being so frightened I forget my name,
think it's yours, that they're the same.
Other rooms will always need skin
but in Heaven I'll give in,

shed all I hide behind: the head full of empty space,
my gallop into The Valley, my Reason Why.
I'll rip up and scatter every verse,
and look at you long then, square in the face.
We have only to die; things have been worse.

Paradise

I've given up arriving, I'll never arrive.
I tried to imagine a way
to enter the room and speak with you,
none are possible. But I still dream of it,

a time and place in me somewhere,
maybe just not ironed or well-lit,
that will turn itself inside out
and let bruised caution drain and heal,

a way of looking at the world not its look,
a way of looking without looking back.
I only dream of it. My green wooden birds,
no longer sad with age, sing in dawn-colored trees

pink-purple as a Persian miniature.
In a flowing castle from a the fourteenth century
we drink coffee and really talk.
The building coils like smoke.

The workers in the fields are not suffering,
no one anywhere is suffering.
The paint, after centuries, is almost dry.
I only dream of it.

A Family Of A Certain Age

A family of a certain age is a confused ghost;
what should be here is not, what's here is strange,
all the more so for seeming right.
It turns a door-knob nowhere near a door,
windows randomly show day and night.

From the front door it used to see places
burned long ago, still glinting in their cracks,
but a Through-The-Looking-Glass fireplace and mantle
bars the way now, smothered in knickknacks
only other people recognize, photos in foreign languages.

What to do but drift through the rooms searching
for doors or someone else, the people it was
in far-off places that looked like this,
see what there is for dinner forever, stand at the mirror,
then cry in the bathroom, writing a poem.

Mermaid

Morning light swims almost through
her bones of milky porcelain,
springy and delicate as a shrimp's coat,
not really out of sight or in,

and the skin above them seems to float on glass:
if she moves her edges glint
like something far-off moving fast.
She watched tv all night, her safe night-light.

Hiding with her are the most-distant movie stars,
the ones about to vanish just from being far away,
who know every secret centimeter
to and from today.

By their light, in her true form
she dances further from death's reach
in a stealthy all-the-time routine
on her remotest, inmost beach.

If discovered she would surely be
imprisoned as a Barnum property,
but here she's safe as a Christmas-tree bulb in June,
no one even looking for the box.

I bring a small breakfast and less talk.
She is grand in her wave-soft chair,
dancing with memory, and for love
I never let on that I see.

Love Poem

Of course we'll die, in the dark
we'll remember there was a planet once
where life pushed sweet, wet fire
through and through a glistening knot

like here, and like here
there was one who loved another
and the other loved that one
and of course they died

everyone died, the planet died,
it was five billion years ago,
and in the dark two particles of dust
collided that became the sun

this planet the sky and our love
that will age to death's best,
secret candy—see what I have,
death will say, come, don't you want it.

Poem At Christmas

You had lights out last year though you were dying;
this year is ending; no one can tell you.
But in my head I do,
without my jets flying,

no covering fire in the air
or mortal stake in argument,
no hurt at you always going where you went.
We talk more now than then, to be fair,

now you're out of crazy games to play,
no spin to lay on the terminal set.
It's worse than useless, being a dead twin.
If you had plans to get away

forget them, there's a lot you should forget.
But you can't go.
I haven't hung lights this year.
My house is a darkness on the snow.

Lord Of Storms

I used to hear you punching clouds
at night, high, far off,
over another people.

Late, late, I'd listen at the dark
to dim, immeasurable events:
proof you were far away

making safe places, punching
clouds away, decreeing avenues,
punching clouds away, planting

housing for us, punching
clouds away unpacking
furniture killing the captives

punching clouds away
I'd be asleep you'd keep punching,
sobbing rare and doubtful words.

You Again

Sometimes, at just a rumble
of hunger from up there,
night would come like you tuned it in
and you'd be stumbling around again
in your invisible upstair
arsenal screaming for blood,
furious, dazzling,
and have us all afraid to die,
struck dumb.

Then bit by bloody bit
your screams would scream outside
and try to get in and get
everybody you hate, or made a peep,
or cried. We'd hide like bait beneath ourselves
dug deep, wetting mud.
The screams were huge accelerating fists
harm grew on like fur.

Once, on a long flight over sea,
I saw how dark it is up there,
how lonely it must be, sad
for shivering angels—and saw too
some clouds are just
breathlike fog! Not, though,
the big blue killers you
shoulder through—such angry air,
setting off all the sirens,
hurting the ground.

I'd always be asleep way
before the end, curled up
and dreaming the storm through,
and in my dreams you'd say
you were my friend, and that
I'd never need a soul but you.

A-9

There was an A-9 Period, the little yellow pills
conned from German pharmacies:
one or two would keep you up all night,
three and you might not sleep right
ever again, so we'd do four with a cheap
Moselle and fare-thee-well.

Spill a bottle: yellow ben-day dots
cartooned the room, rows of shiny
candy suns—an image up-to-date as 1968,
something worth staying up late for—,
and all bright shiny eyes
fixed on those sunny skies.

In every Period since then—war,
better love, better drugs, the bitter
peace of living long enough—
song has been softer and my skin rough,
the deepest part of me still
boiling as then, and the rest chill.

Djinn

The Other Folk look in the window
at yesterday's poem; it's sick
bad, bleeding out on the table.
You did this to me it says.

We did you to you
before you could feel it,
miscarrying a dying heart from room
to room as the light changed
so it could see another sunrise
and sunset, watch a ticking
calendar, imagine its ears empty
of that forever sound.

At one point it cried let me down
and we passed you off
as human.
                    It hurt
abandoning you here
behind the lines; we wept.
We took nothing away,
we earned nothing but these tears
we still share, this
terrifying gliding down
laces tying the world
to pain.
                You are an object
now, frying in time.
You scream in the fire,

29

you can't float here beautifully
as we do. Blame the heart
that caused you if you want if you can;
kill it, get its ashes and eat them,
make sure it's completely gone.

That won't make you better,
won't help at all.
But we want to make things easier for you
and that would make things easier for you.

Rx

Take this pill and Finns have swimming dreams;
these, ice forms in Grecian blood.
That pill, France stares at walls;
those with these and Gypsies
suddenly shudder like horses.

They calm the part of the brain
that imagines it isn't alone,
the sly rider training in dreams
to wake up more adorable,
less foodlike.

There are others in that class:
take this and everyone can read!
Or this one—more your speed—
Christmas on Mercury,
wonderful but over fast.

None of it will help.
You need a world that suffers
an inch for the suffering miles,
ten a day at first then all you can get,
but no one makes them,

no one dreams they could be.
Don't disturb another minute.
You're a grownup and must know now
you are the one wrong thing in the room
and should Go Now.

Shepherd

Now you will shepherd lost things
and they will follow you
through every airport, crowd every interview,
every dinner, every funeral—and follow you,
like it or not, into the smallest hole,
to either pole, ever true.

Tiny cracked angels yanked from the trash
in full song, irreplaceable clear German
marbles, orphaned Army Men;
crystal puppets on dangerous parade,
the logs, the crater and Ray Charles
all only get you to Third Grade.

There was a world to lose then
everywhere crunchy underfoot
—remember that sound?
Now a world has passed all the way through
your slippery heart.
You had a pocket, then a sack,

now you need a Swedenborgian heaven
to keep them all in, a boundless mental situation
where lost things make do
bumping into each other, repeating their names,
watching you.
All to stay until one day

one thing becomes last to lose
and gain the loss of, a final
falling as something unshines,
arrives in heaven dazed, leaking memories.
When that lost thing says hello,
when you pat it on the head

and say what should always be said
in that place where it's alright, airtight
summer and Mom kisses you goodnight,
the herd will scatter, your fadeout event,
going where you were going,
not where you went.

Permament Flaw

Last week you were sixteen again,
late for work that secretly terrified
—such worry about coffee and toast!—,
but now you're much younger somewhere else
and strain for what's redshifted most.

Piglet you cry, and sometimes piteously.
Who is Piglet she's my friend. Piglet,
where are you. Where are we? What sidewalk
or front lawn holds her shed coat and skin?
She's vanished, poor Piglet,

O irreparable loss. This is before years,
a century has yet to bloom.
You float in feelings, and old hurts
are rising from the empty
bottle like a dead perfume.

Wherever this is it's daytime
or you wouldn't be outside
crying for Piglet, worrying
—something's happening she mustn't miss!
You call out as over a terrible cliff.

Before this is a blur of Christmas and wanting.
All red now, too far-off to see,
pulling the world along after
with whatever hurt you, what left you
always trying to escape some doom,

whatever the next doom might be.
That unmendable flaw, where is it,
crazy knowing spider? Not finding
the flaw you know is there is more terrible
than finding it, a doom fit for mythology,

a skill passed through the family.
You cry and reach for a tiny hand
no one can feel or see. When you find Piglet
I hope she says, "Thank goodness oh thank goodness
Betty, thank you for looking, for finding me."

Reunion Tour

In the final dream,
the one for keeps, we climb
up the last time
to where we come clean.

Even memory is numb
up here, every dial on erase.
I think only we have ever come
to this particular dangerous place.

Look: it's a tightrope tour
of what we can't have
in a smart, sticky breeze
—everything but anything below.

For the last time I ask you,
look me in the eye, walk to me.
Last looks are best after,
last looks are as good as they'll be.

Door-To-Door

They say in those days you will pay
for sleep, sleep will be the new gin,
what you need at five-thirty

to help history stop falling
out of photographs, leaping
from burning buildings,

crawling for the exit,
history exploding on the kitchen shelf
hauled off by nameless engines.

You will have all-holiday calendars then,
and clocks showing hours
so late no clock can show them,

and there are fourteen
other things to remember
that everyone forgets.

You have only to look
in their spooky eyes, they say,
to know they have seen things:

Look, I gave up five figures
marketing my family
to carry this message.

Think of me, a former
music-school dean,
are we mad? No

and only those who come along
can go with them
to the moon

where there is so much sleep
we won't ever run out.
Mom and Dad

I gave your car to angels
there's no help for you
goodbye. They say

it's not your fault,
they didn't come for you,
what must happen

to lovers of history
is something best seen
from space.

They say if I miss you,
sleep will be free;
I can dream of you all I want.

I hope I dream of you
as children seduced by history.
You were fine until then.

Young And Dumb

The poem whispers what I should
have said in 1969,
back when the Gods were friends of mine
—not the words I used, that would

only decode in loss, or any
I wanted or needed to speak
(I was dizzy, weak
from wanting so many)

or even the words I thought I'd live,
where free-range terror has an end
and my survival doesn't depend
on a frail gift to forget and forgive.

With each awkward imaginal kiss
I chose against a chance to say
what it whispers now all day:
"It will torment you, remembering this."

It Hurts to Tell You, Hurts To Say

That all has ended,
we have come to the last day,
the party's over,
they forbid display,
the ship has sailed,

each sign says go the other way,
that this was all mischance,
we are farther when we think we're nearer,
we are entirely surrounded by ants,
that every word has long been spoken,

that I broke your image in the mirror
and you whisper through the break
that every reckoning is overdue,
we took every wrong turn we could take,
that there is nothing to recover,

no more turns to make,
nothing to discover,
that we must wake,
that we failed,
that we were our mistake.

The H-Man

The H-Man is eating the Air Base!,
a wave of flesh-eating foam flowed off
the screen, up the sticky aisles
and out the door eating all the way,
rolled over crunchy dustproofed terrain
to Housing—one street gone then one, two,
twenty Loops and Circles
up to where you are until see:
everywhere, all around. In a way,
you understand. He was like us once,
he moves by instinct, driven.

You're ten, you run fast, fast,
watching the world boil off itself into transparent goo,
just about the worst thing that could happen.
You want to reach your family, tell them
Dad! Start the car!
but they're all napping under sunlamps;
no one expects this.
And you run fast, so fast maybe your heart
will explode and you'll be excused,
because he's so much bigger
and faster, inevitable now.

Found Wanting

The air is brightening, another day
is sweeping through. I'd like to say
we're rolling with it, I'd like to say
I'm saying this to you. Things are this way.

And now you've wound up World War II,
light histories of Peter and his dynasty,
Europe's floods of fear and pain.
The grey is shedding a light rain

like tender morning in Germany.
I'm here and there. That's where
we first chewed up the spacy
candy: Edwards, Steiger, Cayce,

and stood in the strange light of fear,
the it-could-be-because-who-knows?
—Kaspar Hauser tries to pick a flame
off a candle, coffins shifting in Barbados—

and the it-could-be-true-couldn't-it?
moronic two and two are fourteen
which is five occult bullshit,
adolescent rage to have the world mean

more than we're told, prove them all wrong,
all that mountainclimbing, chest-thumping
DNA acting-out. I could keep dumping
our authors morning-long:

Velikovsky, true prince of loons,
shameless Churchward, craven Von Däniken,
silly Sommers, that lowly taste for Crowley,
now and then a novel or cartoons...

In all, a misspent reading life, more delight and ease
than substance, but still a life
of books and books shared through that vein
that rendered us inseverably Siamese.

You knew I'd grieve. I'm glad at least
for what you put away, what in the end
you sent from the feast
like an old bad friend, and glad

that for all the wrong books we waded through
it remained when you died still not the moment yet
to open the one on you
about Regret.

Age Of Discovery

For years I thought you off somewhere
flowering from the farthest branch,
breathing just now, yesterday happy or sad,
learning all of age's jokes are bad,

displaced but humming away
sure as a sewing machine slowly running
out of thread. Now the latest report
is, you are dead, dead so long

little remains, your profile gone
from anywhere outside this crayon map.
I used up twenty boxes to show how
things are. All useless now.

On the map you're still OK, supposed
to stay like Eden—there, just closed.
But now I can't tell what's land or water,
where great Persia lies, where my own border.

Everywhere is an empty Quarter.
I'll fill the blank space with armed angels as warning:
back off, stay out, nothing known,
every explorer died alone.

Without Pause Or Doubt

I love a house in Norway
high on a hill in the blue trees,
where the first snow falls.

On a phone ringing for centuries
it calls and calls, it says I'm not there,
where am I? And every century I say

sorry, I was on my way
but drowned, sometimes in Texas
sometimes in Germany underground,

under sea. And you were there for me,
I've kept you waiting all this time
alone by an unringing phone.

Believe I love you, it's me saying so.
I can't tell my windshield what to see.
Believe I love you. Everywhere I go

I haul my longing, I caress
each room and its emptiness,
I fear to lose even what can't be.

And I love you where my road runs out.
Love me there without pause or doubt.

Fragment Of Pausanias

Inside, the temple by the shore
is reminiscent of the National Space And Aeronautics
Museum in Washington, D.C.—large clean spaces
where massive technical devices gleam,
great empty shells.

Marble steps lead from there to the water
and some distance below, where a drowned
veranda overlooks the coastal shelf.
It is said that beautiful Spangdahlem will rise here
from smoking waves.

Some distance off lies a radioactive island,
the surrounding water warm as a bath.
For the second time today I face a shrine
I can't enter. Now the steps are granite, rising to
a burning ghat.

The water rolls off me, racing to be air.
Two men on the well-worn stair are discussing
the newest deadly weapon, atomized computers,
old computers ground to aerosol
that blisters souls.

Back from the beach I return to the temple,
which on this side looks like a manor.
As so often a wrong turn leads me out again,
this time through a maintenance area to a small
instance of lawn.

In the center stands a curious structure of sticks,
a crude, make-do hut bare to sun and rain
and computer fog. In it a grieving prince
awaits the return of the land he prays will
bury this place.

Somewhere Northerly

I am in an airport somewhere Northerly;
students are drinking coffee in small groups
and discussing the odds of our staying overnight.
The building is spacious; someone jokes
we'll each have our own Departure Lounge.
Gradually we drift to the Yoga Center,

which is a bus traveling on a high, narrow road
facing a great river. The views
are spectacular; the driver draws attention
to a row of elegant homes below,
the second-most magnificent owned by an old
rock star we all know is ill, waiting to die.

The road leads to the river
and here we are in the far west of London,
Kingston, maybe. Although it is midwinter
crowds of people are engaged in absurd,
elaborate exercises in the water and I laugh,
reminded of Bosch. There is also a deep pool,

part of the river that ate itself,
where no one is swimming.
Overlooking it stands an ornate Victorian
brick pub, the kind you'd consider
moving to be near. In fact someone asks
if I'm moving here.

Under the pool lies the green tomb
of a pre-Celtic king. I think of him
there stretched out flat beneath armor
and water, waiting to rise.
A rose-bush blooms right in the street.
Every bud opens, gasping for air.

Freeze

You can't have back what you lost to the ice;
your beads are dust, the coat has long regrown
its animals—they've been living on mail
in the basement. What hearts we had
on hand, thawed out, are wet leather bags
the size of babies' fists, no beads
in them stop looking! The Green Man
is in the ground with his good juices,
no beads in the brown fields, no coat,
all edible mail dried up.

You can hide dressed in straw
but when they come upstairs, the nice things
you can't stop missing for a minute,
I hope they find you first and deck you out
in beads bright as an Aztec birthday, wrap you up
in turquoise and jade, fiberglass, anything
to get the cold back in you and keep it there.

Fairytale Ending

There's the house the screams ran out of,
and the dumpster where the body lies.
A drone shot shows how pretty all this looks
from high up in the black skies.

From even higher, an all-white surround:
pale squares on paler ground,
wooded plots the size of a pill,
blue shadows, clots. And from higher still

just stringy roads tossed out
like a crazed hydra-head
grasping fast-food pixels blue and red.
Not a minute now for doubt:

Straighten up, comb and clean,
grab some doughnuts and skip town.
All's quiet as Mom in her Christmas gown,
but from the edges of this midwest dream

it's screams, screams all the way down,
and the road buckles under the weight
of their titanic power and fear.
Never ever has it been so late!

Love or death NOW! Far from here.
One turns the dial, searching for
the perfect score, and the other
suddenly vomits on the floor.

Reciting Dickinson In The Shower

Shine doesn't keep;
it goes right to sleep,
overnight a broken rattlebox thing
in with the hash pipe, hippie beads
and High School ring.

The keepers have dull skin you rub
off against yours slowly
as love and breath wake up
the strobes of their language.
Then one day boom, out of the blue

(west of Australia if they were globes)
a launch of light, then boom another,
another until bloom: the world a rose
of fire, the True moving in with you.
Then you want to hold them all the time,

you see them in the dark through closed eyes,
the only things you care for; showering
you include them and scrub buff gently
as their dazzle nears painfulness, yes,
and never set them by, instead

live with that halo spinning on your head,
a herd of Sputniks blinding the sun.
You will lie dead one day on your bathroom floor,
and for a good while,
because in showering you stared too long at one.

Verse has killed before.
And in its way that will be alright.
There are worse ways to go, we damn well know.
They find you wearing a smile,
smothered in light.

ASP

1. Written With A Broken Wrist

Cruel for wit I could name the cast for you,
diaphanous concrete shelter
capable of smothering a city,
maybe children in the suburbs,
certainly that screaming baby in the bunker.
You are safe in your cold box anyway,
well out of it. You'd never know.

You'd half-deserve it too, oh—you
keeping God's broken bones
safely broken, monster kids in nice clothes
only mothers could love (or make,
I hear you say, cruel for wit).

There are no castles without bad things:
everyone's walked into rooms they never left
or never came out of entirely alive.
We've all lost a ring, a tooth, a token,
been tossed in alchemical drowning pools
where we are silver one day, salt the next.

See? This is the clean white surface
where pain ends, true talisman
against Further Events.
Cartonnage imposes Imhotep's
pure canon on my skin;
the smell of death is troubling

but will wash away.
Osiris is still a dark God.
Beneath this mold an arm is ripening
strong and straight as Pharaoh's.
You lie in your dark place. I'm sorry.
Your ball took a bad bounce.

2. Leonardo's Game

You played Leonardo's game,
the brass ring of seeing
someone we know we know
isn't there, someone in a crowd
invented to receive,

who for you, through a miracle
of control, was never a stranger,
a memory from third grade
dance class, or someone you once
terrifyingly out of nowhere lusted for

on a plane, but he himself,
first of all last things, the one
who'd always been there skating
on a wedding cake alone who fell
and fell, poor plastic groom,

out of a blank sheet of paper
right in your lap without even a stain
to call a body, who you reeled up
through that awful ice
hanging like a king's shroud.

3. Launch It On The Serpentine

Your antique atomizer's just the thing
to boom a paper boat;
you could launch it on the Serpentine,
let go, let it go

like its airplane cousins the optimists
on a stiff, chic breeze. You're down
to the last sheet of paper, the one
you always throw away for luck, lucky you,

and long to christen the Mary Rose
sneezing sweet alcohol
but the cold won't even let you get downstairs
where everything is black ice anyway.

There it lies, dumb oracle,
unlit knowing window
at the bottom of the box.
Rest from such weather is all you can do,

lay a place for the irresistible
ritual, take the silk out for a spin.
The room is cold as a permanent cosmonaut,
your barque narrow and dark.

Penalty Phase

Your eyes are filled with cracked light:
no thought of eggshells,
Spanish leather or Watteau;
the spider-lines on everything
radiate from your gaze

and you must let go
the bandage of sight
you wore in so many hells,
and all the beauty you were smuggling,
secret light of painted days.

Leader Dreams
a script:

"Soldiers, this solitude
through which we go
is I."

     — *De La Mare, "Napoleon"*

The city is beautiful burning, I would stay
to watch but the dogs are anxious,
they know I am always right but are human
anyway that can't be changed
so back into the hole I go to once again
as usual keep everything running.
They want to see me now, all of them,
but what is there to say
I was right all along
we have been betrayed
by our softness.
They want maps, gas,
tanks, embalming fluid, why not
instead why not here I give them
each a plaza named for me
here take it open a coffee-shop
cut hair sell chocolate. A few
I give squares edged with brilliants;
no one can say we don't look our best
down here covered in cement-dust, smoke

Numberless guests have come in
to be near me; here a room
crammed with women living and dead
I won't go into I order tea be sent.
Behind that door so many
my old comrades all mostly dead
I won't see them either.
An orderly whispers, "Stalin has put
a bomb in their heart.
All the von anythings will explode!"
Does he think this alarms me
even with a black sun rising outside
and the phones barely functioning
although cleared of rubbish, carrying
only my voice, my vocal will,
Stalin is nothing to me. That should be clear.
I remember suddenly hearing he died,
yes, long dead
of course he and Rosenfeld drowned in blood
in their mad attempt to cross the ocean
circling the pure Land. The city
is burning why was I thinking
of him? That name is shit on the ground.
I continue my continuous arrival.

It is really Spring in one room
authentic windows everything the mountains
are best this time of year
I walk out on the terrace the sky
is full of plumbing cultural heritage
we must one day dig it all down
after finally throttling madness

out of the world. Selling
newspapers—imagine!—next
will come the Leader dolls,
the Leader postcards, porcelains, enamel spoons
the whole village is here,
they should all disappear.
One of my numberless guests
waves a paper in the air
it can't be the thirty-second another
rushes over do you see? It's
just as you said you are not safe
I give him The Look anywhere I am
is safe perhaps it's you who needs protection.

Abruptly I allow myself to be taken
inside for the other numberless guests
I am furious why are these people
not already out in the sky
inspecting plumbing? I am injected
that I may continue suffering such
cowards to breathe cement.
Who here does not rejoice in this may go
but of course no one leaves,
they applaud, once more I have torn
myself open to feed them, pigs,
filthy calculating animals.
I go around table by table
lighting lamps calling for maps
to burn, all of them, the city
needs reinforcing flame
or all will be darkness.
As usual I am misunderstood,

now everyone is picking up trash.
It's my birthday! There will be a parade
the first of an endless series every town every
stinking crossroads will burn
with torches I am Germany's heart
we have dreamt immortally

Here already from canvas and bunting
they conjure the Kroll Opera, where
one can see things clearly. Speer is painting
a flag on the sky with a severed hand he
has a trainload Heinrich has given
me a flag it's bleeding a piece
is missing he's chewing it Hermann
wipes flag from his lips with a flag
a wolf leans toward me she will almost
reach me if not stopped, rubbing her belly
it's a bomb! And drops
on an Aubusson flag giving birth
to an H, it's broken a beautiful swastika
stillborn. I will hang them all
from it, what the world lost,
poor little black bloody
hook. Someone says it was born
out of time. They are stupefied
when I point out that obviously this is poisoning;
British agents, monsters, babykiller
terror-atrocity-bombers that have crept in

and now they're all looking for poisoners
check the plumbing someone yells
I see smoke they are gassing us it's their last hope

the room is rotating, flames are lining up
to sneak in like traitors. Heydrich
has only reported once since he died,
he carried white flowers.
But here he is now screaming
from his car get in! They have
always, all of them, taken me for a fool.
No, not with you. "But today is the
thirty-second just as ordered,"
he whines. I have the road removed.
He can sit down here with the rest of us
One day I will abolish names
there will only be 'Leader' and 'you.'
Ah, the Philharmonik has arrived

We need more than this, much more,
and because they have not seen it,
not even Heydrich from heaven, I allow
them this once into the gleaming granite
fist of Germania. They were a crowd
but here they are dust.
Hess arrives, he has killed Churchill
through boredom. "My Leader!" he cries.
"Who has ever doubted you?" You
have all doubted me but see!
Look at my hard thought!
Feel the chill of this quarried people!
More people, more men
I cannot wait for the final rally
when I drive victory like a stake
through their throats—they will cheer out blood
then, these cowards wondering about

seating and will maps be provided
with the blank program: "All white!" Joseph crows
in his fool-them-all-but-me mewling
phony man-voice. "All one thing, text
and page and people!" He seems pleased.
I look up to where I shall proclaim
all possible futures: Bormann

After the Fall I will let them all go
they can fly off like birds
greedy puppets, insects
struggling for another day on a dead planet
I have always been too kind, too indulgent
they are bringing in the cake
now, shaped like Germania
smothered in candles and craters
even my cook has abandoned me!
Most likely for Himmler. I look
in the audience he isn't there
none of my iron knights it's getting warm
now, they are off packing
practicing St. Louis accents, buying nylons.
I finger my Party Badge.
Who gives orders here? I shout.
The plumbing is on fire, the fire above
creeps down to the roots
of the people but no one notices.
We will burn alive! I shout
but no one moves, perhaps
taking this for an order. I leave
them downstairs forging maps
on programs with their dirty fingers

Berlin is beautiful burning
the Overture is starting
I will listen from here, watch it
in flames. From the beginning
Gods are equal with their doom.

Changed

My parents had a son;
the Others took him
and put one
of theirs in his bed.

So I am here instead
of who I might have been,
made-broken toy,
blind beddyboy,

twistyface, twitchylimb,
chewed-out heart.
I don't remember when
I wasn't who I had

to be, or wonder how he
is, the other me.
He should be glad;
I've been sad from the start.

Oracle

Up the woods behind the Junior High,
way off the road, sure I was unseen,
I knelt and begged for Poetry.
Quiet as the youngest green.

Then a red flower in the snow,
bright as the gift I prayed
for, launched a Guadalupe glow:
I deserve answers, I'm in Ninth Grade.

A child had lost it, the bright
flower, and touching it I stood
by a great hurt hidden in the wood,
the kind forgetting can't set right.

Unmistakable answer, terrible reply!
And as if I couldn't read the message
or imagine why the rose was there,
I laid it on the grave of my prayer.

From A Line Of Rilke

Now they bring their innerness entirely, express
the inmost wrinkle on the farthest horn,
the hind hoof half-inch longer than its mate,
that anxious, isolate tip of the tail,

and turn a shattered smile to fate,
going through dying as they did being born,
falling taken as minds fail
chewed by the frenzied music of distress.

In the last crumb the whole loaf is sleeping late;
just so, they can ignore the knife and nail
undoing outlines—bloody, beaten, torn,
they smile nonetheless,

as if the death they must adorn
were really a new body to possess,
silent beneath a golden veil,
in a dark grotto, behind a locked gate.

Flood

Sometimes in dreams it rolls back up
to trembling potential, spitting body parts
and house-chips out whole on a contracting path,

straining calm from chaos, zipping it all up,
bigger than life and wider than wide-screen, so seen
and unreachable, hell at any speed,

and you can't stop or slow or turn away from it
all the way to the nightmare end:
coffee brewing, children in warm beds.

Keeping Within The Lines

No parts of us were really the same,
but the resemblance made clear
we had been one thing once,
sharing more than a name.

When you cut off your thumb,
that wrong-way G-chord
thumb, I could never watch you play
again without trembling, struck dumb,

the sight uncanny as a wound on the sky.
That was my thumb, shockingly gone!
I felt guilt. You joked about power tools:
If you can't use them, don't try.

In time that whole body burned. And few
remember when the fire was in you,
but in my charred poundage, ploughing through
these miserable days I do, we do,

now all there is of you is me,
half-vacancy,
and all there is of us
dust, brother, dust.

Long, Long

Sorry to hear about your dad,
that had to hurt. Bad, bad.
And the wife you ran away,
she coming back? Not today.
Or the children? No.
And the farm? Even so.
And you. Long ago.

Tamara In The Green Bugatti (1925)

Ninety years later only my hat
is wrong–imagine that! I should
look odd as La Pompadour to you
or what's a future for? What did you do,
how did you lose the future I drove to your cradle,
how did you break it, that dazzling toy?
I meant you to go so far…sad boy,
in a hundred years I couldn't say
how beautiful this looked from far away.

Sadness Comes Out Of Me

Sadness comes out of me as the sea,
as snow, pines, grey November skies,
as broken fences. Why these images
are feelings I don't know,
I only know what they mean to me. Maybe

the poem instructs me: "See?
Don't fool yourself, you're sad.
That flowering peach
is really a pine, it's a late-November
afternoon, and however hard you worked

to picnic in the sun day is done,
fences broken and buried in snow,
you're underwater and need to know."
Be quiet poem, leave me my tree.
I know what comes out of me.

Uncalendared

Grabbing dark cold outside,
now a room blitzed by giftwrap,
put that wet jacket somewhere—on the balcony
is fine, make sure it doesn't blow away.
For an hour at end of day

Suffer this practical alchemy,
called from routine
as to once-a-year prayer.
Ignoring it's a bad mistake to make,
compounding loss, so I have come to visit where

they bake the cookies I don't bake,
give the ghost of childhood control,
listen to Bing and Nat King Cole
and lay out bowls of tangerines,
nuts, gold-wrapped chocolates

—anything that doesn't glow
good to eat. Here they tag the days
and watch the holiday rise
through the calendar as a square blaze,
warm and right. They're entitled to say no

to winter-dark, Christmas-cold. The Void
throws Whistlers at the window.
Outside my jacket shivers with light.
I will wear the season's Text,
false flowers tiny, hard, and bright.

When they darken I'll just be a cold man,
no ideas attached to make a way,
only memorized motion in a dark maze.
I take light where I can
because night is dark, and day.

It was stupid, walking. And my house is far away,
dark as a cathedral, wrapped in cold
that can be heard, where my bed
or bier is slight, off in a corner
out of sight, unlisted, uncalendared.

Ghost

Even the language knows you're not there;
we say "the ghost of X" not X,
what starts at X'd end.
You aren't a parent or a friend

or the Grey Lady on the stair,
but at best a glowing shadow cast
by something far away in strange light–bright
air, no presence or past.

Be off from troubling me…
you could more usefully be
elsewhere curved in a glowing spark,
blowing on an eyelid in the dark

to show you're more than this: a hurt of memory
—a mind outside, scratching to get in.
And I beg you, since you can't tell me so,
tell them I still love you and you still know.

Pietra Dura

Here is the closed blue eye of time
you touch to make sure, to see.
Through a flat window of stone
they pass a rose of lapis lazuli,

pale stem and leaf of jade,
the long wide opal sky lit
low to the left, which must be West.
Flat stone. The rose can barely fit.

Day is done, they want you to dance,
maybe more if you read the message there
or see how they move through thick evening
and smile. The rose hangs heavy in the air,

thick velvet dampening your skin,
and whatever the angels intend
you reach out your hand again
and say yes, drag me in.

Raised In Captivity

Your shadow is a black wedge
on the snow, its own canyon,
blisteringly deep. Like certain scenes of history
the sight of it kills. You will fall in, simple hiker,
raised in captivity, for all your skills.

From every angle nothing but edge!
Raised in captivity, for all your skills
the sight of it kills. You will fall in, simple hiker,
and burn as you fall. Like certain scenes of history
—asteroids all—it brings its own canyon,

a sign saying run, the end of history.
You cast a perfect permanent canyon
on the snow, simple hiker.
Nothing for miles but that black ledge
and you, raised in captivity.

Pilot

My brother is a pilot in the dream. We are on a withered plain
looking into the distance. His nearby jet is capable
of interstellar travel and he is leaving on a long flight.

I am in a car then driving on a busy street
in south Austin full of people heading to
a festival. It's warm; they wear little but masks.

And everything is perfect in its way: we are busy as a nightmare
row of registers on a holiday; I look carefully and there
is nothing here remotely like unending night.

Vanishing

Those children on the stair,
see them? Nothing there. Yesterday
I saw a bird vanish. Not fly away,
just gone—dark air,
dark wings.

I'm seeing things,
nothings that come and go;
already I half-understand
almost not being there,
not quite being at hand.

They come and go, glimmering.
I don't care about the return;
I want to know
—before I learn—
about vanishing.

Notes

"Door to Door" appeared in *MAGMA Poetry*, 2012.

"Leader Dreams", "Pilot", "Somewhere Northerly", and "Fragment Of Pausanias" first appeared in *96th of October*, Summer 2021 and Winter, 2022.

"Raised in Captivity" appeared in *The High Window*, Spring 2021.

About Atmosphere Press

Atmosphere Press is an independent, full-service publisher for excellent books in all genres and for all audiences. Learn more about what we do at atmospherepress.com.

We encourage you to check out some of Atmosphere's latest releases, which are available at Amazon.com and via order from your local bookstore:

Melody in Exile, by S.T. Grant

Covenant, by Kate Carter

Near Scattered Praise Lies Our Substantial Endeavor, by Ron Penoyer

Weightless, Woven Words, by Umar Siddiqui

Journeying: Flying, Family, Foraging, by Nicholas Ranson

Lexicon of the Body, by DM Wallace

Controlling Chaos, by Michael Estabrook

Almost a Memoir, by M.C. Rydel

Throwing the Bones, by Caitlin Jackson

Like Fire and Ice, by Eli

Sway, by Tricia Johnson

A Patient Hunger, by Skip Renker

Lies of an Indispensable Nation: Poems About the American Invasions of Iraq and Afghanistan, by Lilvia Soto

The Carcass Undressed, by Linda Eguiliz

Poems That Wrote Me, by Karissa Whitson

Gnostic Triptych, by Elder Gideon

For the Moment, by Charnjit Gill

Battle Cry, by Jennifer Sara Widelitz

I woke up to words today, by Daniella Deutsch

Never Enough, by William Guest

Second Adolescence, by Joe Rolnicki

Made in United States
Orlando, FL
19 June 2023

34290606R00061